summersdale

SOPHIE GOLDING

YOUR POCKET CHEERLEADER
TO HELP YOU THRIVE

BE YOUR BEST SELF

BE YOUR BEST SELF

Text by Miranda Moore

An Hachette UK Company
www.hachette.co.uk

Summersdale Publishers Ltd
Part of Octopus Publishing Group Limited
Carmelite House
50 Victoria Embankment
LONDON
EC4Y 0DZ
UK

www.summersdale.com

Printed and bound in China

ISBN: 978-1-80007-161-2

Substantial discounts on bulk quantities of Summersdale books are available to corporations, professional associations and other organizations. For details contact general enquiries: telephone: +44 (0) 1243 771107 or email: enquiries@summersdale.com.

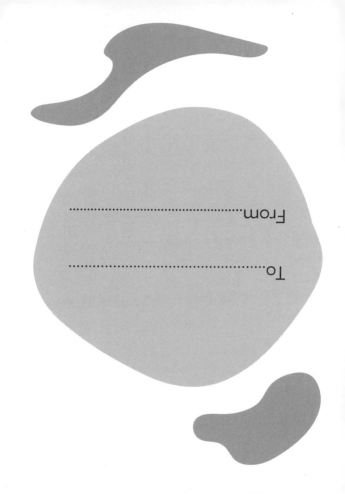

To ....

From ....

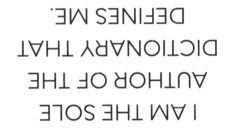

I AM THE SOLE AUTHOR OF THE DICTIONARY THAT DEFINES ME.

Zadie Smith

INTRODUCTION

This little book is here to empower you to make positive changes in your life, as well as remind you how great you already are! By learning from past mistakes, choosing positivity and keeping your focus aimed forward, you'll be well on your journey to finding purpose and contentment.

Of course, there's always room for a little self-improvement, so if you're motivated to become the best possible version of you, dip in and heed the wisdom of the voices in these pages. And if you're usually your own worst critic, it's time to learn to accept yourself for the wonderful person you are.

BE YOURSELF

You are the number one
person in the world at being
you. Be proud of who you
are and always stay true to
your character and principles.
Instead of chasing each and
every passing trend, set your
own standards, stand up for
what you believe and follow
your passions. It will earn you
the respect of others, as well as
boost your own sense of self-
worth. In short, don't try to be
someone else; instead,
be your best self.

CREATE THE HIGHEST,
GRANDEST VISION
POSSIBLE FOR YOUR
LIFE, BECAUSE YOU
BECOME WHAT
YOU BELIEVE.

Oprah Winfrey

Little things to remember

Out of almost eight
billion people, you are
the only, unique *you*

MY APPROACH IS JUST FEARLESS. I'M NOT AFRAID TO TRY ANYTHING.

Stormzy

WHAT DO
YOU LIKE
MOST ABOUT
YOURSELF?

I WILL NOT FOLLOW
WHERE THE PATH
MAY LEAD, BUT I WILL
GO WHERE THERE IS
NO PATH, AND I WILL
LEAVE A TRAIL.

Muriel Strode

REACH FOR YOUR DREAMS

Have the courage to reach for your dreams, however big and wild they may seem. Even if you don't achieve them, you'll get a lot closer than if you never try in the first place – and you might well gain greater self-esteem and a sense of satisfaction in the process.

"

IT'S EASIER TO
MAKE YOUR WAY
IF YOU GET TO
CHOOSE YOUR OWN
SOUNDTRACK.

Fredrik Backman

HOW CAN YOU BE A BETTER FRIEND?

NO ACT OF KINDNESS,
NO MATTER HOW
SMALL, IS EVER
WASTED.

Aesop

Little things to remember

Self-criticism gets
you nowhere; self-
improvement gets
you moving forward
with purpose

WHEN YOU CAN'T
FIND SOMEONE TO
FOLLOW, YOU HAVE
TO FIND A WAY TO
LEAD BY EXAMPLE.

Roxane Gay

YOUR BEST SELF

Describe the very best version of you. What matters most to this very best self? Would you be proud to call this person a friend? Consider: how does this differ from the person staring back at you in the mirror? Commit to one or two small changes to make your better self a reality, but be kind and reasonable in your expectations; nobody is perfect.

I WANT THE WORLD TO BE BETTER BECAUSE I WAS HERE... I WANT IT TO MEAN SOMETHING.

Will Smith

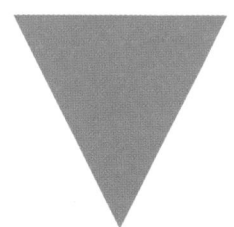

Little things to remember

Perfection is a myth;
you can only be your
best self

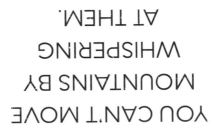

YOU CAN'T MOVE
MOUNTAINS BY
WHISPERING
AT THEM.

Pink

WHAT GREAT
THINGS HAVE
YOU ALREADY
ACHIEVED?

SET GOALS

Put a little thought into working out what it is you really want to achieve – it could be a small thing you wish to do today, something in the next year or a long-term life goal. Don't settle for friends' aspirations; set your own – and don't be afraid to be ambitious. Setting daily, weekly or monthly targets and planning how to achieve these can help to keep you focused and on track.

"

THE ONLY WAY TO
DO GREAT WORK IS
TO LOVE WHAT YOU
DO. IF YOU HAVEN'T
FOUND IT YET,
KEEP LOOKING.

Steve Jobs

HOW MUCH TIME
DO YOU DEVOTE
TO THE THINGS
YOU LOVE?

I AM
STRONGER
THAN FEAR.

Malala Yousafzai

Little things to remember

Recognize, deep in your soul, that you are an excellent person

YOU CAN'T LET
YOUR FAILURES
DEFINE YOU. YOU
HAVE TO LET YOUR
FAILURES TEACH YOU.

Barack Obama

BE ACCOUNTABLE

Try not to blame others for things that don't go your way. Carrying around bitterness gets you nowhere. If things aren't going as well as you'd like, instead of wasting energy on resentment, think of ways in which you can make adjustments and improvements, and then be accountable for these. Freeing yourself from the habitual blame game can be enormously liberating.

THE MOMENT WE DECIDE TO FULFIL SOMETHING, WE CAN DO ANYTHING.

Greta Thunberg

Little things to remember

Make time for the activities
and people that give you
the most joy

WHAT MADE YOU SMILE TODAY?

I CAN'T GIVE YOU A
SURE-FIRE FORMULA
FOR SUCCESS, BUT
I CAN GIVE YOU
A FORMULA FOR
FAILURE: TRY TO
PLEASE EVERYBODY
ALL THE TIME.

Herbert Bayard Swope

Little things to remember

All those little things you've achieved over the years? Add them together and see how far you've come

IF I CAN HELP ONE
PERSON, AND THAT
ONE PERSON CAN
HELP ANOTHER
PERSON, THEN IT
BECOMES A CHANGE.

Kakenya Ntaiya

WHAT SMALL
ADJUSTMENTS
COULD YOU
MAKE TO YOUR
DAILY LIFE
THAT WOULD
POSITIVELY
IMPACT THE
WAY YOU FEEL?

PRACTISE POSITIVITY

Think of your energy as being contained within a tank. Positive thinking generates energy and fills the tank, while negative thinking drains it. Spend a day making only positive or neutral observations and comments, even if it feels contrived. See how much better you feel afterwards. You are simply learning to see and respond to things in a constructive way, and will hopefully feel more energized as a result.

COURAGE DOESN'T ALWAYS ROAR. SOMETIMES COURAGE IS THE LITTLE VOICE AT THE END OF THE DAY THAT SAYS I'LL TRY AGAIN TOMORROW.

Mary Anne Radmacher

Little things to remember

The year ahead is not yet written, so become the author of your own destiny

WHO IN YOUR
LIFE MOST
NEEDS YOUR
SUPPORT, AND
HOW CAN
YOU HELP?

CHALLENGE YOURSELF; IT'S THE ONLY PATH WHICH LEADS TO GROWTH.

Morgan Freeman

HELP OTHERS

Helping others is pretty much guaranteed to fill your life with purpose and satisfaction. By donating your time, skills and energy – particularly to those less fortunate than yourself – you will be exercising your finest human trait: compassion. In a world so driven by efficiency and economic value, altruistic acts are a significant demonstration of generosity and goodwill.

THE BEST WAY TO FIND YOURSELF IS TO LOSE YOURSELF IN THE SERVICE OF OTHERS.

Mahatma Gandhi

HOW CAN YOU
SPREAD KINDNESS
IN YOUR LIFE?

COMPASSION ISN'T
ABOUT SOLUTIONS.
IT'S ABOUT GIVING
ALL THE LOVE THAT
YOU'VE GOT.

Cheryl Strayed

Little things to remember

Prioritize your physical
and mental health
to help you achieve
greater balance in life

REMEMBER THAT
YOUR BODY IS A
VESSEL FOR THE WILD,
EXTRAORDINARY
THING THAT LIVES
INSIDE YOU.

Nikita Gill

BE AUTHENTIC

Avoid striving for some artificial measure of success or perfection. What is success, anyway? Is it looking flawless, with a glamorous job, dream house and extravagant possessions – all subjective concepts anyway? Or is it having close friends, being genuine and making your unique contribution to the world? Be yourself, seek authentic joys and don't buy into glossy ideals. You will find greater satisfaction in that than in any stereotypical notion of success.

WE MUST
ROW IN
WHATEVER
BOAT
WE FIND
OURSELVES
IN.

Christie Watson

Little things to remember

Effort, commitment and passion matter more than results

I JUST ASPIRE TO BE
THE BEST I CAN BE. I
WANT TO WORK HARD
AND SET ONE GOAL AT
A TIME FOR MYSELF.

Bella Hadid

WHAT DO YOU
VALUE MOST
IN LIFE?

I HAVE JUST THREE
THINGS TO TEACH:
SIMPLICITY, PATIENCE,
COMPASSION. THESE
THREE ARE YOUR
GREATEST TREASURES.

Lao Tzu

DO WHAT YOU LOVE

Various adages promote the value of doing what you love and loving what you do, and they share a universal truth. First, though, you have to discover what it is you love. Ask yourself: what are your greatest strengths? What are you passionate about? What makes you feel useful? If you can dig deep into your psyche and do things that match your values and skills, you'll experience greater fulfilment in life.

IF YOU BELIEVE IN
YOURSELF ANYTHING
IS POSSIBLE.

Miley Cyrus

WHAT IS YOUR HAPPIEST MEMORY?

Juan José Méndez
Fernández

DON'T TELL
ME YOU
CAN'T.

Little things to remember

Your friends love you just as you are

THERE IS NO MAGIC
TO ACHIEVEMENT. IT'S
REALLY ABOUT HARD
WORK, CHOICES, AND
PERSISTENCE.

Michelle Obama

MAKE IT HAPPEN

It's all very well having a grand vision, but to make it a reality you need to break this down and tackle one thing at a time. Is there some specific behaviour, interest, activity or attitude you'd like to work on? If so, further dissect and scrutinize this idea. What practical steps can you put in place to make it happen? Sketch out a plan and commit to it.

THERE IS NO WAY AROUND THE HARD WORK. EMBRACE IT.

Roger Federer

Little things to remember

You are a somebody;
you matter

I'M INTIMIDATED
BY THE FEAR OF
BEING AVERAGE.

Taylor Swift

WHO IS YOUR
NUMBER ONE
CHEERLEADER?

I AM A GREAT BELIEVER IN LUCK. THE HARDER I WORK, THE MORE OF IT I SEEM TO HAVE.

Coleman Cox

SPEND YOUR TIME WISELY

It's up to you how much time you allocate to different elements of your life. If you feel swamped with too many chores and don't have enough time for the fun stuff, decide what is truly necessary and prune back other activities until you have a good balance. What can you delegate, or even delete off your to-do list altogether? This can make space for new interests, to help you make the most of your time.

WHAT ARE YOUR
ASPIRATIONS,
BOTH LARGE
AND SMALL?

IT'S TAKING
SOMETHING THAT'S
A NEGATIVE AND
TURNING IT INTO
A POSITIVE.

Megan Giglia

Little things to remember

Sometimes you have to swim upstream to reach your destination

I'M PROUD OF THE WAY I'VE DEALT WITH SETBACKS. IT'S HARD WHEN YOU FEEL DOWN... BUT YOU HAVE TO PICK YOURSELF UP AGAIN.

Jessica Ennis-Hill

APPRECIATE FRIENDS

Think of a friend or relative who always has your back. What could you do to show them how much you appreciate their support? Make time for that special person – surprise them with something thoughtful, or clear space in your diary just for them.

YOU'RE TOUGHER THAN YOU THINK YOU ARE, AND YOU CAN DO MORE THAN YOU THINK YOU CAN.

Christopher McDougall

Little things to remember

Positivity attracts people
like bees to a flower

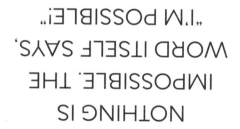

NOTHING IS IMPOSSIBLE. THE WORD ITSELF SAYS, "I'M POSSIBLE!"

Audrey Hepburn

WHO DO
YOU MOST
ADMIRE IN LIFE
AND WHY?

IF YOU DON'T TRY
THINGS AND TAKE
RISKS, YOU DON'T
REALLY GROW AND
FIGURE OUT WHAT
YOU WANT.

Zendaya

Little things to remember

Be curious and marvel at the world around you

IF YOU WERE
GIVEN A FINITE
WINDOW OF
TIME TO ACHIEVE
SOMETHING,
WHAT WOULD
YOU CHOOSE
TO DO?

DON'T SIT DOWN
AND WAIT FOR THE
OPPORTUNITIES TO
COME. GET UP AND
MAKE THEM.

Madam C. J. Walker

CELEBRATE LITTLE WINS

If you make a point of marking every success (however small) for yourself, as well as for close family and friends, you're setting up a helpful habit of celebrating life's ups. Whether it's an assignment completed, a personal best or a difficulty overcome, it reminds you to value life's little wins. Why only acknowledge major accomplishments, such as graduations and awards, when regular small celebrations help keep you motivated and grateful?

THE MORE YOU PRAISE AND CELEBRATE YOUR LIFE, THE MORE THERE IS IN LIFE TO CELEBRATE.

Oprah Winfrey

Little things to remember

Life is too short to tread water; you have to choose to swim forward

WHAT ARE YOU GOOD AT?

CONTENTMENT IS
A STATE OF THE
HEART, UNAFFECTED
BY OUTWARD
CIRCUMSTANCES.

Crystal Paine

BE KIND

Kindness is contagious. If somebody is kind to you, it lifts your spirits and inspires you to be kind, too. And if you do something kind for another person, they may well pass it forward. Demonstrate kindness today and you will likely feel better about yourself, as well as brightening the day for others. After all, being kind costs nothing but creates a sense of immeasurable wealth.

REMEMBER TO LOOK
UP AT THE STARS
AND NOT DOWN
AT YOUR FEET.

Stephen Hawking

Little things to remember

Never underestimate
the extent of your
numerous talents

HOW CAN YOU MAKE TIME FOR THE ONE PERSON IN YOUR LIFE WHO IS ALWAYS THERE – YOU?

BE BRAVE. TAKE RISKS. NOTHING CAN SUBSTITUTE EXPERIENCE.

Paulo Coelho

FIND YOUR PURPOSE

If you seek satisfaction and purpose rather than success, you will paradoxically be more likely to succeed. Doing activities and work that you find enjoyable, satisfying or fulfilling on some level means you'll naturally want to stick at it and will have the inbuilt motivation to keep improving. And you may as well succeed at something you love, rather than just succeeding at something!

REMEMBER THERE'S NO SUCH THING AS A SMALL ACT OF KINDNESS. EVERY ACT CREATES A RIPPLE WITH NO LOGICAL END.

Scott Adams

Little things to remember

Always make time for good friends – listen to them, support them and make them feel valued

IF YOU CAN DO
WHAT YOU DO BEST
AND BE HAPPY,
YOU'RE FURTHER
ALONG IN LIFE THAN
MOST PEOPLE.

Leonardo DiCaprio

WHAT
ARE YOUR
WEAKNESSES,
AND WHAT
STEPS CAN
YOU TAKE TO
OVERCOME
THEM?

LEARN FROM FAILURES

We all have past regrets and failures – the trick is not to allow yourself to be weighed down by them. Now is the time to move on. Perhaps you will fail again, but that's OK. By learning from failure, you will become stronger, and the only way you can ever succeed is by trying again.

HOW WONDERFUL IT IS THAT NOBODY NEED WAIT A SINGLE MINUTE BEFORE STARTING TO IMPROVE THE WORLD.

Anne Frank

CAN YOU
DESCRIBE YOUR
BEST QUALITIES
THROUGH THE
EYES OF A
FRIEND?

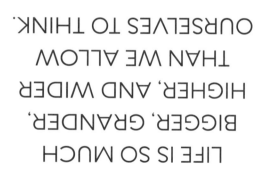

LIFE IS SO MUCH
BIGGER, GRANDER,
HIGHER, AND WIDER
THAN WE ALLOW
OURSELVES TO THINK.

Queen Latifah

Little things to remember

Express gratitude every day for the things that are good in your life

IT TOOK ME 17 YEARS AND 114 DAYS TO BECOME AN OVER-NIGHT SUCCESS.

Lionel Messi

BE DISCIPLINED

All the great sports stars will tell you they reached the top of their game by putting in years of hard work. If you wish to reach a goal in life, being disciplined with your time will give you that structure and focus to make it happen. Set parameters for yourself and stick to them. Adjust them as required until it feels like a healthy, sustainable balance.

Little things to remember

Forgive yourself and others for wrongdoings, slip-ups or errors; we all make mistakes

STAY STRONG, BE BRAVE, GO BEYOND.

Cristiano Ronaldo

HOW CAN
YOU STAY
MOTIVATED
TO ACHIEVE
YOUR GOALS?

I THINK AS HUMAN BEINGS OUR KINDNESS IS WHAT DISTINGUISHES US.

Ziauddin Yousafzai

GET UP EARLY

If there's a particular goal you wish to achieve, but you feel you just don't have the time, you could commit to getting up an hour earlier than usual each day to work on it. If you keep it up for a month, you'll gain 30 hours to devote to this aim! Imagine how great you'll feel afterwards, having achieved something you simply couldn't find time for before.

UNTIL YOU MAKE
PEACE WITH WHO
YOU ARE, YOU'LL
NEVER BE CONTENT
WITH WHAT
YOU HAVE.

Doris Mortman

WHAT DREAMS
HAVE YOU YET
TO FULFIL?

Little things to remember

Your time is precious – it's OK to say no sometimes

DON'T BE PUSHED BY
YOUR PROBLEMS. BE
LED BY YOUR DREAMS.

Ralph Waldo Emerson

HAVE ASPIRATIONS

There is nothing self-serving about ambition. You only have one life, so it makes sense to make your time count. Why be mediocre when you could be great? Really think about what you would like to achieve in your lifetime. Seek out inspirational people and read memoirs of success stories. Drive, focus and perseverance will help you realize your aspirations, whether they are modest or grand.

Little things to remember

You are worthy of respect

YOU HAVE TO BELIEVE
IN YOURSELF WHEN
NO ONE ELSE DOES –
THAT MAKES YOU A
WINNER RIGHT THERE.

Venus Williams

ARE YOU
CONTENT
WITH YOUR
WORK-LIFE
BALANCE?

SMILE!

When you smile at a stranger, it can make their day – and yours! So practise smiling more, even if it feels contrived at first. Research shows that smiling tricks your brain into actually feeling happier, so when you smile, you start to feel better. What's more, if people mirror your behaviour and smile back, you can create a loop of goodwill.

THERE IS NO ELEVATOR TO SUCCESS, YOU HAVE TO TAKE THE STAIRS.

Zig Ziglar

WHEN WAS THE
LAST TIME YOU
VISUALIZED
YOURSELF
ACHIEVING
A SPECIFIC
OBJECTIVE?

Little things to remember

Every day provides a
fresh opportunity to try
something new

EMBRACE FRESH CHALLENGES

We all know someone who is perfectly nice, but who always sticks with convention and is afraid to try new things. Do you want to be that person? If you would rather be someone who embraces challenges, have the courage to commit to that choice. Your life will become immeasurably enriched by new connections and experiences as a result.

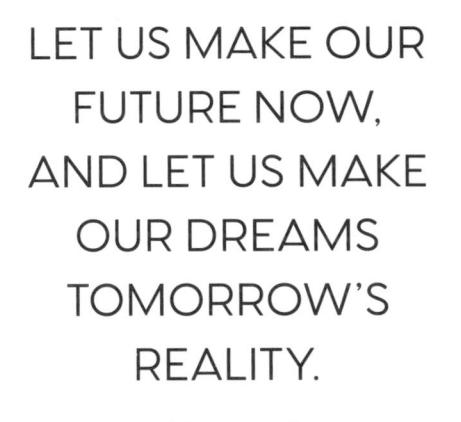

LET US MAKE OUR FUTURE NOW, AND LET US MAKE OUR DREAMS TOMORROW'S REALITY.

Malala Yousafzai

Little things to remember

Nobody else's skill set matches yours exactly, so embrace your unique talents

WHAT COULD
YOU DO
TO MAKE
TOMORROW
MEMORABLE?

EVERYBODY HAS A
UNIQUENESS AND
EVERYBODY'S GOOD
AT SOMETHING.

P!nk

BE CURIOUS

Being curious means engaging with the world and showing respect to the people and things around you. Imagine you are a small child, seeing and experiencing things for the first time. Carry this spirit of wonder with you for the rest of the day and see what marvels you notice when you really open your senses and soul.

WHAT WOULD
YOU LIKE TO BE
REMEMBERED
FOR?

IT'S EASIER TO GO DOWN A HILL THAN UP IT BUT THE VIEW IS MUCH BETTER AT THE TOP.

Henry Ward Beecher

Little things to remember

Your strengths far
outweigh your weaknesses

WHAT ARE YOUR GREATEST PASSIONS?

CURIOSITY ONLY
DOES ONE THING,
AND THAT IS TO GIVE.
AND WHAT IT GIVES
YOU ARE CLUES ON
THE INCREDIBLE
SCAVENGER HUNT
OF YOUR LIFE.

Elizabeth Gilbert

Little things to remember

Believing in yourself is
more than half the battle

LOOK AFTER YOURSELF

Make time for your physical and emotional well-being. Plan how you can fit in regular exercise, write a schedule and stick to it – a fitness app can help to keep you motivated. Eat plenty of fresh fruit and veg, prioritize quality sleep, and think about the actions that will support your mental wellness, such as practising mindfulness and spending time in nature. Life is invariably better when we feel energized and nourished.

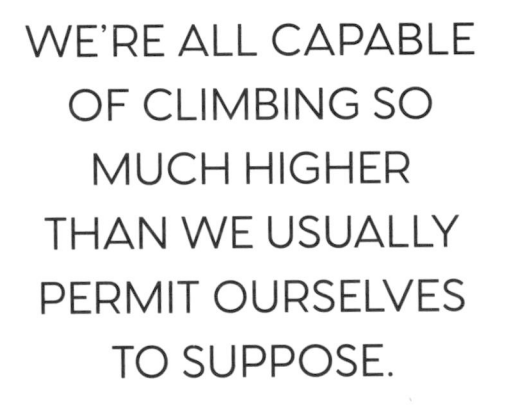

WE'RE ALL CAPABLE
OF CLIMBING SO
MUCH HIGHER
THAN WE USUALLY
PERMIT OURSELVES
TO SUPPOSE.

Octavia E. Butler

HOW COULD YOU
MANAGE YOUR
WEEK TO MAKE
MORE TIME FOR
YOUR INTERESTS?

THE MINUTE
YOU LEARN TO
LOVE YOURSELF,
YOU WOULD
NOT WANT TO BE
ANYBODY ELSE.

Rihanna

Little things to remember

Always say sorry if you've done something wrong, and accept apologies from others trying to make amends

NEVER STOP BELIEVING IN THE POWER OF YOUR IDEAS, YOUR IMAGINATION, YOUR HARD WORK TO CHANGE THE WORLD.

Barack Obama

KEEP FIT

The World Health Organization recommends adults should do a minimum of two-and-a-half to five hours a week of moderate-intensity exercise – ideally more, for additional health benefits and to counteract sedentary lifestyles. In addition, it recommends muscle-strengthening activities involving all major muscle groups at a moderate to high intensity at least twice a week, together with less time spent sitting. So dig out your sports shoes and have fun getting active!

YOUR TIME IS LIMITED,
SO DON'T WASTE IT
LIVING SOMEONE
ELSE'S LIFE.

Steve Jobs

Little things to remember

You are CEO of your own life

YOU DON'T HAVE TO BE ANYTHING BUT YOURSELF TO BE WORTHY.

Tarana Burke

WHAT IS YOUR BEST PERSONALITY TRAIT?

BE PROUD OF
WHO YOU ARE.

Eminem

ACCEPT YOURSELF

One of the greatest things you can do to be the best you is to accept yourself exactly as you are. Valuing yourself and being content with your lot are two of the great wisdoms of a fulfilling life. Not everyone's ideal is to be famous or world-class at something. Learning to be less self-critical and more self-accepting can do wonders for your contentment, and it will rub off on those around you.

IF WE DON'T TRY, WE WON'T KNOW.

Ellen MacArthur

WHAT DO YOU BELIEVE IS THE FINEST HUMAN QUALITY?

DO WHAT YOU LOVE.

Andy Murray

Little things to remember

Set your own standards; don't settle for other people's

IF YOU'RE TRYING
TO BE SOMETHING
YOU'RE NOT, IT'S
SLOWLY GOING TO
BITE YOU IN THE BUTT.

Bella Hadid

PRACTISE GRATITUDE

Gratitude is strongly correlated with a positive mindset, so develop a habit of conscious gratitude for all the good in your life. Express this by writing down three things you're grateful for each day, or by acknowledging them out loud, and always thank people for their contribution, however small.

"

Little things to remember

Set aside time for yourself each day

I DON'T
THINK LIMITS.

Usain Bolt

WHAT ARE
YOU LOOKING
FORWARD TO
TODAY?

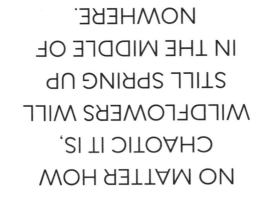

NO MATTER HOW
CHAOTIC IT IS,
WILDFLOWERS WILL
STILL SPRING UP
IN THE MIDDLE OF
NOWHERE.

Sheryl Crow

VISUALIZE YOUR DREAMS

Close your eyes and let your
mind take you to a place where
you feel fulfilled, purposeful
and comfortable. Really inhabit
this place in your imagination,
where you feel fully yourself,
fully alive and fully engaged.
What is it about this picture that
is appealing to you? Consider
changes you could start putting
in place now, in order to make
this vision your reality.

WITHIN YOURSELF THERE'S A TALENT, A GIFT, A PURPOSE THAT NEEDS TO BE FULFILLED AND YOU NEED TO DO IT.

Stormzy

Little things to remember

The world is better
because you are in it

YOUR VICTORY IS
RIGHT AROUND THE
CORNER. NEVER
GIVE UP.

Nicki Minaj

WHAT SMALL
CHANGES WILL
HELP YOU
BECOME YOUR
VERY BEST SELF?

WE ARE WHO WE CHOOSE TO BE.

Will Smith

Have you enjoyed this book?
If so, find us on Facebook at
Summersdale Publishers, on
Twitter at **@Summersdale** and on
Instagram at **@summersdalebooks**
and get in touch.

www.summersdale.com